Warning:

The information in this publication is for educational purposes only. In no event shall the author be held responsible for misuse of this book and its contents.

Guillaume Lemagnen

Demystifying Ninjutsu, a Necessary Task

Introduction

Ninja and *ninjutsu* present a great paradox because they are so well-known and yet so misunderstood.

The proof of this point lies in the fact that *ninja* and *ninjutsu* are always viewed in the context of research into budôka (the practitioners of *budô* such as *karate, jûdô, aikidô,* etc.) but nothing could be further from the truth.

The reality is that modern *budô* was created during the 19th and 20th centuries and represented a shift from martial disciplines to sporting practices, and thus have nothing in common with the thousand-year old traditions employed during centuries of warfare.

It is therefore very important, if not essential, to recall that *ninja* and *ninjutsu* come from another culture and another land : namely Japan, a country with very deep historical, social and cultural differences and only superficially 'Westernised' until recent times.

It is obvious that not everyone can understand and engage with *ninja* and *ninjutsu* because they are the cultural manifestations of a different society, so research must be carried out by others. Japanese specialists in history, ethnology etc ... , are best placed to do this.

It is an observable fact in the West, even if it is only grudgingly acknowledged, that almost anyone can claim a complete knowledge of ninjutsu or set himself up as a *ninja* expert. This deplorable situation has existed for about fifty years.

In order to clarify matters I have written this book. During its preparation Mr Jinichi Kawakami, a specialist in *ninjutsu* and honorary director of the *Iga-Ueno Ninja* Museum and special professor at Mie University came to hear of my work. Taking an interest in my efforts Mr Kawakami offered to correct my work. This book is therefore the first in the Western world to be supervised and corrected by the world's expert on ninjutsu. All my thanks got to Mr Kawakami for the time and energy he devoted to this humble work.

All errors and mistakes, needless to say, are my own responsibility.

Guillaume Lemagnen

Summary

Ninjutsu today and its origins

Contemporary *ninjutsu*

Looking back, two books alone were sufficient for the *ninja* to become world famous :

- «You Only Live Twice» by Ian Fleming (1964).

- «Shôgun» by James Clavell (1975).

Both were written by British authors, and it was their movie adaptations (in 1967 and 1980 respectively) that provided the basis for the *ninja* craze. Their strong image made a deep and lasting mark and spread widely on an international basis.

«Shôgun» takes place during the feudal medieval time around the beginning of the Edo Period (c. 1600). The story includes a *ninja* squad besieging a castle where the hero is located.

«You Only Live Twice» sees the famous secret agent James Bond having a brush with *ninja* sent to assassinate him in modern Japan. The Japanese government also supply *ninja* to help his mission.

These movies represent the first face to face contact between *ninja* and the West, where he appears as a black-clad nocturnal killer.

Although works of movie fiction, this image would dominate the public imagination, leaving historical reality far behind. The public took it on board and for many years ninja have been seen as amoral secret assassins.

It may have been an unflattering portrait but the infatuation by the public for this image of the *ninja* was immediate and started the western trend (first in America and then in Europe) between about 1970 and 1990 with the so-called «*ninja* boom».

During this time the ninja inevitably invaded the media with varied results. One may recall :

In comics : Frank Miller's creation of Elektra involving *ninja* women wearing red clothes and in a direct parody of Elektra Kevin Eastman and Peter Laird created Teenage Mutant Ninja Turtles. Even Batman is trained in the *ninja* tradition in some versions of his story because he is an expert infiltrator and can fight, spy and escape under cover of darkness.

As for the cinema, The Cannon Company with their actors Michael Dudikoff, Steve James, Sho Kosugi and Chuck Norris produced many films about *ninja* including the Famous «American Warrior» series. Many films came from Hong Kong as normal Asian movies involving scenes with a Western actor wearing a *ninja* costume, all aimed at the American market.

We must now consider an important point. When the *ninja* boom was at its peak many people naturally wanted to study *ninjutsu*, the art of the *ninja*.

Indeed, parallel to the ninja boom this time was marked by the remarkable popularity of Bruce Lee in the West as the same public discovered the martial arts. Martial Arts and *budô* were known about at this time but it was nothing compared to what was to happen as the success of the «little dragon» movies provoked a martial frenzy all round the world. *Dôjô* and martial arts clubs were created and spread like wildfire offering *karate*, kung-fu, *jujutsu* etc…

At this time, amid ignorance of Japan and ignorance of what *ninja* really were the logical situation demand that *ninja* should have their own martial discipline or martial art. Just as a *judoka* practised *judô* and a *karateka* practised *karate*, surly there must be a «*ninjutsu-ka*» ?

Ninjutsu might also be assimilated as a simple fighting technique, albeit a little different. It was also inevitable that it should also be considered as an art of assassination because the only view the Western world had of *ninja* was as an assassin.

More importantly, many people wanted to learn this concept of *ninjutsu* because it was seen as producing invincible warriors with mystical powers.

The demand was considerable and so was the supply that followed in response, but we can immediately appreciate two major obstacles:

1. *Ninja* and *ninjutsu* came from Japan, representing a huge cultural difference from the West (a gap of space).
2. *Ninjutsu* and *ninja* had long since passed into history (a gap of time).

However, these details were not seen as a problem by the *dôjô* that sprang up from nowhere whose masters claimed they were taught by masters of the *ninja* tradition, although offering no proof for this.

In the best cases they provided a mixture of *judô*, *aikidô*, *karate* and so on, the Japanese nature of the disciplines suggesting that *ninjutsu* was very close to the mix.

In the worst examples the instructors mixed up everything with scant regard for the truth, combining *kung-fu*, *tai-chi*, *qi-gong* from China with other disciplines that had no links to Japan.

In those teachings they used the name *ninjutsu* with no questions asked about its authenticity.

Ignorance of *ninjutsu* therefore paralleled its popularity. Even today it is a rag-bag of numerous mixed disciplines. Moreover, with its connotation as the «art of the assassin» it inevitably attracted the wrong sort of person.

Anyone who seeks to learn assassination must have mental or moral weaknesses, making them a danger both to themselves and to others.

What happened was that acts of aggression were performed by people dressed in *ninja* clothing as in the American movies. This was very bad publicity for the reputation of *ninjutsu*. Thus it was that the *ninja*-boom temporarily disappeared some time around 1990.

Nevertheless *ninja* retained a place in the popular imagination because of the impact they had made as popular icons, hence the new success *ninja* enjoyed at the dawn of the millennium.

Once again American cinemas took the lead with new titles like «Batman begins», «Ninja» or «Ninja Assassin». The latter title show stat in spite of the passage of many years the concept of the *ninja* had not evolved at all.

Now we can see that the popular image of *ninja* is one frozen in time. It has become a stereotype and stereotypes do not exist in historical reality and truth.

So what is important to bear in mind ?

First, wo must understand that *ninja* and *ninjutsu* came to the public's attention through Western movies not Japanese ones and that these representations tended only towards the spectacular and the sensational. This misshapen vision was far from historical truth.

Secondly, these movies gave *ninjutsu* a reputation as the art of assassination, which attracted unethical and psychotic people trying to make money from the *ninja* boom for their own interests, and this tendency still persists today. The misshapen perception of the *ninja* inspires ann modern representations and always in spectacular fashion.

It was the initial aim of this book to describe ninja in the West and to appreciate how wrong it is. Ninja and ninjutsu came from Japanese history, so that must be our starting point as we go back to the origins.

The origins of *ninjutsu*

It is quite common to hear of *ninjutsu* as being a «dark art», and there are indeed elements of this through the influence they have had on Japanese history. Indeed the *ninja* conformed to this reputation for invisibility by leaving few tracks of his existence.

This was chiefly because *ninjutsu* was an oral tradition. It is no secret that even in Japan today many people doubt their existence, regarding them as just a myth.

Yet the myth has a basis in legends, and the first had a decisive role in the founding if the Japanese empire.

Jimmu Tenno (Emperor Jimmu) is a legendary character and the descendant of *Amaterasu* the goddess of the sun, according to the most ancient Japanese written records (the *Kojiki* and *Nihongi*, written during the eighth century). By virtue of his divine inheritance he was the founder of the Japanese empire and its first emperor, seven centuries BC.

While his power was still being established *Jimmu* did battle with a rival at Iso Castle, but the fight went against him. One night he had a dream of collecting clay from the holy mountain of *Amenokaguyama*, modeling it into a cup and presenting it to the gods. The dream appears to be an excellent omen, so *Jimmu*'s hopes rose.

But *Amenokaguyama* was behind enemy lines and it was not possible to mobilise men who were close to surrender to collect mere clay. So two of his faithful servants, set their minds towards accomplishing this dangerous mission. Using the disguise of non-threatening farmers they managed to cross the enemy lines, collected clay from the mountain and brought it back safely to their master. *Jimmu*, following his vision, made a cup to dedicate to the gods and win the battle, and thereby imposed his supremacy and his divine lineage on Japan.

That is of course just a legend. The two servants were not *ninja* and in fact *ninjutsu* was born many centuries later. But at least the spirit of *ninjutsu* was present : A mission was accomplished without the use of force but instead by employing ruse and deception without being noticed : The conduct of *ninja*.

Because the principles of *ninjutsu* are universal and thousands of years old, such strategies of diverting one's enemies attentions elsewhere, secret observation, escape have been employed since the beginning of humanity, and many animals too have a natural capacity for camouflage.

As noted above, *ninja* and *ninjutsu* are areas that require great care because there are few surviving accounts or records. The accounts appear later in Japanese history (in the *Kojiki* and *Nihongi*) the first books written in Japan) and the events of previous times were not valued.

Yet we can relate in great detail the story of *ninja* and *ninjutsu* activities

It is recognised that the cradle of *ninjutsu* is the historical region of *Iga* (伊賀) and *Kôka* (甲賀) (now within the prefectures of *Mie* and *Shiga*) ; more precisely *Nabari* (名張). And *Kôka* was part of *Iga* at this time.

Lake *Biwa* once occupied the area now known as *Iga*. As it shifted to its present location it changed the nature of the soil, leaving *Iga* poor for cultivation. Its inhabitants quickly realised that agriculture was problematic and there was little yield in spite of all their great efforts.

So they had to turn towards another source of income. In fact, the majority of the early inhabitants of *Iga* were *hakuto* (outlaws) accustomed to hiding, spying and flight, and this role would have led towards espionage. It was a useful skill-mix.

Nara and Kyoto, the successive capitals of Japan, were near to *Iga* and *Kôka* and therefore ensured that the *ninja* would have continued employment.

Because they were self reliant and had such an ingenious capacity for survival, the application of these skills led to exceptional political independence. *Kôka* and *Iga* had not submitted to the authority of a *daimyô* (local lord) instead *ninja* families lived independence lives until the *Sengoku* Period.

Other residents were immigrants leaving their home countries for Japan but perhaps failing to integrate into Japanese society and taking refuge in these wild and inhospitable regions. They brought their own knowledge, spirituality rituals and esoteric knowledge. These would give birth to a syncretism and these exchanges of knowledge benefitted *ninjutsu*.

Mention is often made to «The Art of War» by Sun Tzu (c. 500 BC) being the origin of *ninjutsu* because it includes a chapter about spying. It is highly unlikely that people of *Iga* knew of this book when they took up their spying activities so were therefore not influenced by it. «The Art of War» was not studied deeply in Japan until the *Edo* Period and *ninja* used spirituality in their craft, which is contradictory to the purpose of the book. «The Art of War» therefore had no influence on *ninjutsu* or *ninja*.

Heian Period (794-1185)

It is likely that it was during this time that *ninjutsu* took shape in *Iga* and *Kôka*, which suggests that *ninja* families are already established there.

Sengoku Period (1467-1603)

This period is known as the *ninja* golden age. It was a time of war and conflict when the art of *ninjutsu* became essential for all the warlords. Violence, rivalry and suspicion were rife. Law lay with the strongest and it was not a good idea for a *ninja* to be too clever ; some *daimyô* were paranoid and tried to eliminate this highly skilled element.

And yet this time saw the fall of *Iga* when the war destroyed it. This event was the *Iga no Ran* (the *Iga* Revolt). Oda Nobunaga, Japan's first unifying general, set out with 45,000 troops to curb the insolent independence of the *Iga* families. *Iga* had only a few thousand to oppose him and after fierce resistance *Iga* fell, unleashing a general slaughter of the population. Perhaps half died. Systematic execution and pillaging broke down the prosperity and liberty of *Iga*.

Soon afterwards the death of Nobunaga provoked new internal squabbling. One of his lieutenants, Tokugawa Ieyasu, had to cross the *Iga* region to rally his forces. He received help from the *Iga* and *Koka* ninja and crossed the region without hindrance. This service would not be forgotten.

Edo Period (1603-1868)

This period began by the taking of power by Tokugawa Ieyasu who acquired the title of *Shôgun* (military commander) and made *Edo* (modern Tokyo) his capital. Japan was pacified after incessant wars. Tokugawa Ieyasu hired many men from *Kôka* and *Iga* as his secret police, placing Hattori Hanzo in charge of them.

Yet this favourable development marked the decline of the *ninja* communities because their services were not needed in a time of peace. The arts and training of *ninja* and *ninjutsu* were gradually abandoned.

Most importantly, from the *Edo* Period onwards spying became a job for samurai and samurai had to adapt to their new role. Seeking employment, the *ninja* would try and promote his services by publishing written works, although suitably falsified of course to preserve the real *ninja* secrets.

At these same time he would approach samurai for employment, sharing with them some knowledge of spying and strategy to benefit the samurai tradition, trying to prove that the knowledge would be useful to them.

It is important to note that even if spying skills were passed on to samurai they would still be simple spies, not *ninja*. *Ninjutsu* was a tradition passed on within families and it was out of the question to share it with a foreigner.

Most interesting of all is the fact that at they same time as they disappeared the *ninja* became famous in Japan through *kabuki* plays and *ukiyoe* prints. It was not necessary to be accurate about them, and indeed some *ninja* families exploited this.

Showa Period (1926-1989)

This was the last time that activities relating to *ninjutsu* can be recognised because some knowledge persisted and was taught as espionage techniques during World War II. At this time the word «*ninja*» started to become popular.

So what is important to bear in mind ?

The important point is that historically the *ninja* was not a warrior but a spy so by using stratagems and camouflage he avoided fighting. Long periods of warfare served the *ninja* families well, but they were also dependent upon war, so when Japan was pacified *ninjutsu* was progressively lost and its place taken by a myth created and propagated by popular culture.

A Japanese print representing Jiraya on a giant frog he had conjured up to fight. This illustrates every well the modern idea of ninjutsu where the ninja is seen as rewarded with magic powers. In fact Jiraya was not an adept of ninjutsu but of yôjutsu (magic). Ninjutsu and yôjutsu were combined during the Edo Period in representation of ninja.

The etymology of «*ninja*» & «*ninjutsu*»

Nowadays the word «*ninja*» is known throughout the world, but is in fact a modern creation, like «*ninjutsu*».

In ancient times he was frequently known by his place of origin such as *Iga mono* (man of *Iga*) or *Kôka mono* (man of *Kôka*).

At various times in Japan some secret operatives were called 'grass'… (etc.……). However this does not specifically denote a *ninja*, merely one who carries out a certain task. These names are very expressive about their activities but were not formal names for *ninja*, even is he performed these activities.

The modern use of *ninja* dates from the beginning of the 20th century.

The term *ninjutsu* (忍術) was current during the *Edo* Period, although the characters were read as «*shinobi jutsu*» and the characters for *ninja* (忍者) as «*shinobi no mono*». Reading them as *ninjutsu* and *ninja* are modern developments.

Nin (忍) means secrecy, endurance etc,

Jutsu (術) is art, skill or technique.

Ninjutsu is called the art of spying in Japan, a discipline that is discrete and secret ; but we should avoid this definition because in reality *ninjutsu* has to be understood as the totality of knowledge, skill, strategies and habits to accomplish missions.

The «*ninja*» kanji (忍) are read «*shinobi*» when alone and «*nin*» when combined with «person» (忍者).

The «*nin*» character (忍) combines sword (刀) with heart (心) ; a sword under the heart as in the Sword of Damocles.

Secrecy and the ability to withstand pain : A definition of a *ninja*. This can be acquired through *ninjutsu* training, after that a person deserves to be called a *ninja*.

The term «*ninpô*» (忍法) appeared in the *Edo* Period too and denoted the phantasmagoric image of the *ninja* as wizard on prints and in the theatre at that time.

Ninja, the adept at ninjutsu

When the question of ninjutsu is discussed it must first be appreciate that it is an essentially secret tradition. So researchers have to work from ideas and small fragments of knowledge. A harder task is to separate fact from fiction, but gradually the truth about ninjutsu is revealed giving us a clear picture of the tradition.

Born a ninja

Historically, to be a *ninja* means to have been born and raised within a *ninja* family.

Japan was a land separated into different castes (nobles, warriors, farmers etc.) with each having its own laws, codes and traditions. But the caste of *shinobi* was not officially recognised within society at that time. Because *ninja* lived at the margins of society and people had no idea of their existence except for those hired their services. It is interesting to see that this transmission of secret techniques was through specific families in a hereditary manner. We must remember that *samurai* and *ninja* were separate categories.

Today we can see from a family name if an ancestor was linked to *ninjutsu* and it is not surprising to identify this as a separate hereditary caste.

Not everyone was a *ninja* within a *ninja* family.

To become a *ninja* was difficult and reserved for those few would could achieve and sustain that stays. Those not selected in the family would probably help in other way by supplies, etc.

Any village connected with *ninjutsu* would have the normal daily round of pottery, weaving etc,

Ninja also used as a cover professions like medicine sellers or artists, and many years if practice made him skilled at the domain he chose. It was also a job he could pass on to his descendants. The *Hattori* family was well known in the *Nô* theatre.

The *ninja* hierarchy

Ninja are usually described as being subdivided into three levels :

- *Jônin* (上忍) superior ninja rank.

- *Chûnin* (中忍) middle ninja rank.

- *Genin* (下忍) inferior ninja rank.

In reality this is a recent invention based on a personal interpretation of *Mansenshukai*.

Ninja would have existed in a hierarchy, but not enough details are known about it.

Even descendants of ninja families have no answer. Any hierarchy was probably based on filial obedience of common decision making, but nothing can be said for certain.

Ninja ethics

Contempt and scorn for ninja by *samurai* is well-known in Japanese culture.

It is often suggested that the sense of ethics specific to the *ninja* did not meet the criteria in vogue among the *samurai*, moreover, in fact they regarded *ninja* as cowards devoid of honour.

We can see here a representation of opposite values of opposite characters ; *ninja* and *samurai*.

This was somewhat subjective and maybe reveals a little jealousy, but the efficacy of *ninja* was recognised by those who hired their services, yet it continues today in the unconscious image of the *ninja* in Japan and in foreign countries. It can be explained by the opposition between the two sets of values.

Under the influence of *Edo* Period values a samurai was viewed as the loyal servant of his lord and worthy in all circumstances. He would never disgrace the reputation and honour of the master whose badge he wore on his clothes.

These values explain why is it considered than *samurai* rejected *shinobi* actions such as operating in the shadows, avoiding confrontation, hiding and using strange ways to achieve his goals. *Ninja* and *samurai* did not follow the same moral code.

Yet there was no contradiction with *samurai* values in the fact that that the *ninja* acted with total devotion to his mission rather than to his lord!

Ninjutsu was based on survival because a *ninja* was not allowed to die until he had accomplished his mission. So a *ninja* could run, flee or do any number of appalling things to achieve his objective, and he did not care what *samurai* thought. He was not afraid to die but his total motivation was to complete his mission.

The *ninja* had no ego : Prestige and honour meant nothing to him, indeed he had to reject those notions because both were incompatible with the spirit of *ninjutsu*. Neither did money, food or sex work for him, and no ninja tried to avoid being scorned. There is evidence indeed that he didn't care about it because *ninja* honour was always located elsewhere.

Ironically, a *samurai* of the *Edo* Period placed in charge of spying and information-gathering activities would himself have to reconcile his principles with tasks he judged to be infamous.

Training and formation

Belonging to a *ninja* family was one thing ; to become a *ninja* was quite another. As ninjutsu was transmitted by heredity, it was a gruelling training he would suffer to make him into a *ninja*. The status was praiseworthy but attained by very few.

In many of its aspects *ninjutsu* training is a mystery, leaving the door open to many invented theories.

In fact *ninja* training was very hard and reserved only for an elite.

The selection of a *ninja* started at birth ; the child would be constantly yet discretely evaluated as to his dispositions, personalty and character : the criteria for selection.

A child with their requisite capacities could be declared fit to start training, and he was selected at about 5 or 6 years old.

He could be trained to dislocate his joints so that he could worm his way in to narrow gaps or simulate infirmity.

Every day he would improve his jumping by jumping over an ever growing plant or out of hole that he would dig deeper every day.

His developing strength meant he could extricate himself from any situation. He would have to run long distances tot flee quickly or carry messages.

Psychologically the *ninja* learned to cope with many privations such as hunger, thirst, heat, cold lack of sleep.

He endured pain by rejecting his ego.

His severe training brought him to a mental state that led to the gate of *Fudôshin*, one of the most important aspects of mental training.

He practised concentration to develop his energy and his will.

He trained his five senses until he could hear a failing nail or see in the dark.

He trained his memory to retain informations.

He became a skilled conversationalist so as to manipulate and acquire information.

All along he applied these to specific situations, aiming to develop his ingenuity and capacity to improve.

From a cultural point of view a ninja acquired much wide knowledge and learned to read and write, normally a high class privilege.

He would familiarise himself with the lifestyles of the other classes to pass himself off in any disguise on his missions.

He familiarised himself with dialects to avoid arousing suspicion when he crossed distant lands.

In general he learned what men are, their different characters and motivations in order to manipulate them.

Survival was a very important aspect of *ninjutsu* so he learned strategies of fleeing and surviving in the natural environment.

He learned about edible and inedible plants and how to use poisons and medicines from them.

He knew how to test the ground and see how people had passed that way.

Another part of his training was dedicated to science, learning chemical reactions and using it for his own benefit, such as gunpowder.

After a dozen years of this he could be considered a *ninja*.

It was this specific training that placed him out of the ordinary in society.

We must appreciate that *ninjutsu* was much more than just a simple collection of techniques but a group of knowledge that distinguished him for the common people by the amount of knowledge he acquired.

The important parts of ninjutsu are :
- The development of physical capacity
- Survival skills
- Deep psychological knowledge
- Ingenuity and scientific rigour that was way ahead of his time

The *ninjutsu* diet

Ninjutsu training was focussed on physical and mental abilities, but a *ninja* had to stay slim and alert to be efficient. To achieve this objective *ninjutsu* developed a suitable diet as part of ninja life.

Ninja had a deep knowledge of diet drawn from his own observations and it played a part in the formation of *ninjutsu*.

In Asia diet is an intrinsic part of spiritual development, hence the inclusion in *ninjutsu*.

In Japan, Zen monks practised «*shôjin ryôri*» : Diet for spiritual health and development. This diet excluded all meat and anything of animal origin. It was strictly vegan and came from the Chinese Buddhist dietary tradition.

In order to understand the *ninjutsu* diet some cultural and historical facts should be appreciated.

Historically the Japanese ate vegetables and very little meat. The Chinese book «*Gishiwa ji den*» (-300 b.c), describes Japan as a country whose inhabitants consume little meat.

With the import of Buddhism from Korea, Japan adopted a diet very close to the vegan.

In 675, Emperor Temmu banned all animal products from alimentation.

In 737 Emperor Seimu authorised the consumption of fish and sea food, but it was usually eaten only during festivals.

These principles stood until the *Meiji* Era, during the Tokugawa Period an edict banned the consumption of pork and beef.

During the *Meiji* Era with the introduction of a western lifestyle meat eating began in Japan.

During the *Edo* Period white rice was a luxury ; ordinary people ate brown rice and legumes. The spread of white rice dates to the end of World War II.
Brown rice is complete rice including the bran with higher level nutrients.

The *ninja* foods were closer to the traditional Japanese diet but with variations.

Cereals, especially rice, form the basis of most Asian diets, but in the *ninjutsu* diet rice was consumed raw or not at all. First because rice growing was difficult in the *ninja* lands and second because rice was high in calories and a *ninja* would avoid this sort of food and despised luxury, preferring a more stoic food.

Soya is an essential part of Japanese food culture and is eaten every day. However in Japan it is not eaten in its natural form but changed under the Chinese Buddhist tradition to *tofu*, *miso* or *shôyu*.

For vegetables and wild plants there were carrots, daikon, Chinese cabbage, burdock, turnip, lotus and bamboo roots, mushroom, pumpkin, mountain greens, spinach, melon etch and many Japanese plants (pasanie, kaya, gumi, ...)

Seeds, nuts and sesame seeds are importants too.

Japan is also famous for its consumption of seaweed (kombu, wakame). Omnipresent in soups they are also dried to preserve them and to cure ailments.

Vital in Japanese cuisine are pickles (*tsukemono*). Meat consumption being unusual, vegetables are pickled in salt. There are many types. *Umeboshi* (salted plums) are regarded as being very health going and clean the blood.

That said, *ninja* had an interest in so-called black foodstuffs: black rice, black sesame seeds, black beans, black tofu etc. In Japanese tradition black foodstuffs were good for body care and spiritual development and as such were part of *sennin shoku* (hermit diet)

The *ninjutsu* diet ruled the following items out completely :
- Meat : Excluded from traditional Japanese diet already, the consumption of meat was regarded as impure, bad for the health and polluting the blood, interfering with «*ki*» (energy) and reduced one's spirituality considerably. Also meat eating caused a strong body odour, so *ninja* would avoid this.

- Garlic : Garlic was viewed like meat and not eaten even by vegetarians in Japan. Garlic was also excluded form *shôjin ryori* for the same reasons.

- Onion : Mainly avoided to reduce body odour.

- Alcohol : Because it hindered reflexes and balance a *ninja* excluded alcohol, although everywhere in Japanese society, a *ninja* was training to resist intoxication.

The cooking methods would be the same as in traditional Japanese cuisine ; everything was warmed to a minimum level to preserve the quality of the ingredients. Uncooked items are considered good for spirituality (as in *shôjin ryôri* and *sennin shoku*).

During missions, a *ninja* would avoid lighting a fire so as not to be noticed.

In the *ninjutsu* diet, as with all Japanese cooking, one avoided being sated so as not to become sleepy.

Also, the *ninjutsu* diet included the preparations of food rations. These are low calorie but able to remove pangs of hunger and thirst and gave energy; they came from the military world but were developed by ninja.

The rations were mad into little balls about 1 cm in diameter, easy to carry and to eat. Recipes and preparation modes are as numerous as the usable ingredients

Hyôrôgan (兵糧丸) ; ration pills

A mix of brown rice, buckwheat seams seed with sake or black sugar. These are true emergency rations.

Kikatsugan (飢渇丸) ; rations for hunger or thirst relief

Cereal flour mixed in sake with vegetables (eg carrots, wild plants), used to relieve hunger and thirst.

Suikatsugan (水渇丸) ; thirst relief rations

Mix of umeboshi, black sugar, molasses and mushrooms, used to relieve thirst.

This scrupulous attention to the ninja's diet shows very well that ninjutsu is not a technique but first of all a healthy lifestyle. This is very necessary in the application of *sanmunin* (see next section).

Sanmunin

Because the art of *ninjutsu* is based on secrecy, a *ninja* must be invisible in all his activities when on a mission of infiltration. For this he resorts to *sanmunin* (三無人) ; cover one's tracks in three ways.

If not being seen or heard is vital for spying, being able to hide one's body odour is equally important. More exist, but the three following principles ware both basic and necessary

Don't be recognised (無色)

A ninja would use a disguise (see later chapter) or wear local style clothes so as not to stand out from the crowd. Sometimes for missions or night time travel he would wear dark clothes. It may surprise people to hear that black clothes were excluded, but in fact black shows up very well at night, particularly under moonlight, so grey, brown or dark blue are preferred colours because they blend into the darkness very well.

These night clothes are called *shinobi shôzoku* (忍び装束), a modern name. They allowed freedom of movement and there was also a *tenugui* (scarf) to cover the face if necessary, but contrary to popular belief, this was the exception. Also concealing ones face was not unusual in Japanese society, during cold spells for example.

Don't be heard (無聲)

Avoiding noise is fundamental for a *ninja* entering somewhere in secret and he was trained to move silently. This included many types of silent walking techniques.

He also learned to control his breathing and not be given away by it even when physically stressed.

When faced by a noisy obstacle such as a door he would use oil to lubricate it and something sticky to cover the sound of sawing. If he could not avoid making a noise he would create a diversion.

Don't smell (無臭)

Hygiene is very important to all Japanese people but especially for *ninja* who took care not to emit any noticeable odour, so he regularly washed both his clothes and himself.

As noted earlier the *ninja* followed a specific diet to increase his capabilities. Another aspect of this was to remove body odour so that he blended in and would not be noticed by either humans or animals.

A *ninja* excluded certain foodstuffs from his diet for this reason, As noted, meat pollutes the blood and provokes changes in body and sweat odour. Garlic, onions, leeks and spices are excluded to mask body odour as well.

Tobacco and alcohol were rules out on moral grounds but they also had a bad effect on body odour as the *ninja* knew well.

Ninja yashiki

Ninja yashiki (忍者屋敷) is a modern term to designate a ninja's house. It would look quite normal from the outside and nothing would lead to it being distinguished from a another Japanese house, but that was an illusion.

When examined closely the houses were always chosen for the strategic advantages they provided using the surroundings as a natural defence.

Inside the ninja house held many hidden places. A normal house would have just one level, but ninja houses had hidden floors where weapons could be hidden along with equipment and even people. The attic would be used for gunpowder production.

Ninja houses also included traps in case of attack such as pits or trap doors. Because they were built by ninja there were also emergency exist for a rapid escape such as secret passages and tunnels.

Nowadays a few *ninja yashiki* survive but are often in a neglected state condemned to demolition.

Ninja equipment

A shinobi is a spy who has to be secret by nature. Also his equipment did not include weapons at first, just ordinary tools. That explains why weapons were not the solution for a ninja; they were often modified into weapons. This is an overview of at the equipment used by a nina during his missions

Shinobi rokugu, the six *ninja* items

A *ninja* on a mission could not take along any weapons or equipment that would give him away if he was body-searched. That is why he made weapons from tools.

But there are six common items recommended for a *ninja* to bring with him. They are ordinary items but can be used in other ways without provoking suspicion.

It was usual to carry such items so that the *ninja* was not distinguishable from a normal person. He knew how to obtain or create the particular tool.

The six items were grouped together as the *shinobi rokugu* (忍び六具), the usual six *ninja* items.

They are as follows :

- *Amigasa* (編み笠) ; straw hat

Used to protect against bad weather and to cover the face. Some types covered the entire head with a hole to see through.

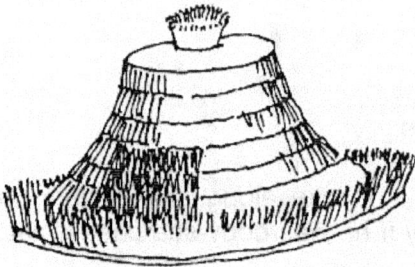

Model of *amigasa*, notice the hole for eyes

- *Sekihitsu* (石筆) ; writing set

A calligraphy set with an ink stone, for messages and also as a hand weapon.

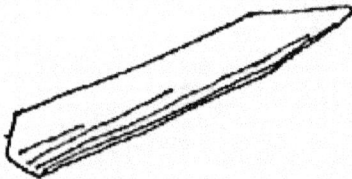

Sekihitsu, stone for writing

- *Sanjaku Tenugui* (三尺手拭) ; scarf

3 *shaku* (1 *shaku* = 30cm) in length can be used in various ways: to cover the face, filter waterer, tend wounds or strangle and enemy.

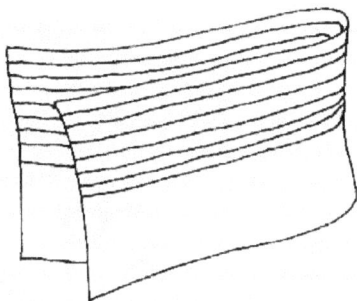

Tenugui, scarf

- *Inrô* (印籠) ; medicine box

A box of small compartments for holding medicine, rations or poisons.

Inrô, medecine box

- *Uchidake* (打ち竹) ; warmer

Made of bamboo and containing embers. Use for lighting a fire or keeping warm.

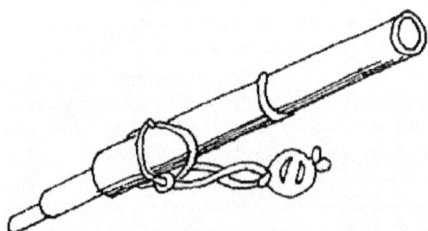

Uchidake, portable warmer

- *Kaginawa* (かぎ縄) ; grappling rope

A long rope with a hook for grappling, climbing walls and trees also to tie someone up or make a trap.

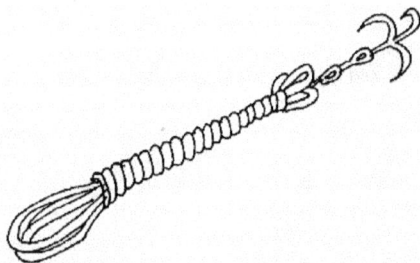

Kaginawa, grapnel

Kunai

Kunai (苦無), «the tool of overcoming problems».

The word indicates the versatility of this item, scratching a wall, loosening boards, making holes, creating steps during climbing etc there were no limits to the possibilities and a *kunai* could have many shapes and forms. In emergency it could be used as a weapon, although not primarily because it was not very sharp.

Models of *kunai*

Armour

The *ninja* was not a warrior so few opportunities arose for wearing armour. Also because of the stress on physical agility armour was a constraint even if it protected him.

But a ninja would train in armour to improve his strength and jumping skills.

The *ninja* of course preferred armour that allowed freedom of movement, so chain mail, *kusarukatabira* (鎖帷子), or leather and chain mail mixture, *karutagane gusoku* (カルタ金具足), but apart from during training armour wearing was the exception.

Armour, models that ninja should wear

Makibishi

The *makibishi* (撒 き 菱) is a pointed tripod called a caltrop in Europe, which was planted in large numbers to cover escape or prevent pursuit. It was of a specifically pyramidal shape where the tip is still pointing upwards.

It is native to China and used in Japan because Japanese sandals were usually made from woven straw, The *makibishi* easily pierced the feet of pursuers.

It is interesting to note that this is probably an observation from nature that is directly responsible for the creation and use of *makibishi*, by providing similar instruments, such as chestnut husks. In Japan, we find also varieties called *hishinomi* (ヒ シ の 実), chestnuts and can be used in a similar use. The *makibishi* is ultimately an improved version of what nature provides.

The *tetsubishi* (鉄 菱) is a model made of iron, stronger, with larger and more pointed tips and was very effective.

The *makibishi* was used on the battlefield, it was not an exclusive tool for *ninja*, if indeed it was actually used by them.

 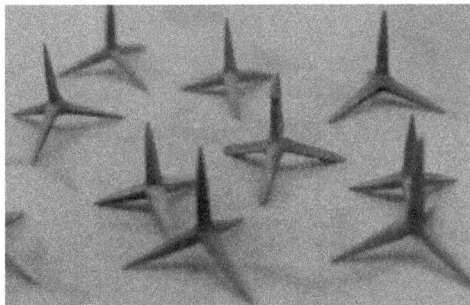

Hishinomi   *Tetsubishi*

Shinobi flute

Shinobibue (忍び笛), a flute is an excellent musical instrument but *ninja* modified it for his own needs ; by adding a section it could become a blowpipe or a tube for breathing under water.

The familiar type was a shakuhachi when in disguise as a *komusô* (虚無僧), zen mendicant monk. Specific tunes and notes were used as code.

Infiltration tools

Ninja capacity included entering buildings in secret, so he had a large collection of tools for this.

Shikoro

Shikoro (しころ) a saw for infiltration or sabotage. Traditional Japanese doors were closed with a latch or a wedge, so instead of breaking it down it was better to saw through the latch.

A flat saw could be inserted into the small space between the door and the frame. With its oval shape a *shikoro* could be used to attack a surface directly and create an opening.

Of course there were many different of models of different sizes depending on the nature of the obstacle.

Shikoro models

Tsubogiri boring surface

Tsubogiri (坪錐) is a tool used to make a hole in something.

A wooden handle was attached to the ring of a tsubogiri and then the tip applied to the surface to makes incisions and create a hole.

Like a shikoro many sizes existed for different diameters of hole. The smallest made a small spy hole ; the large allowed the passage of an arm to unlock a door or steal something.

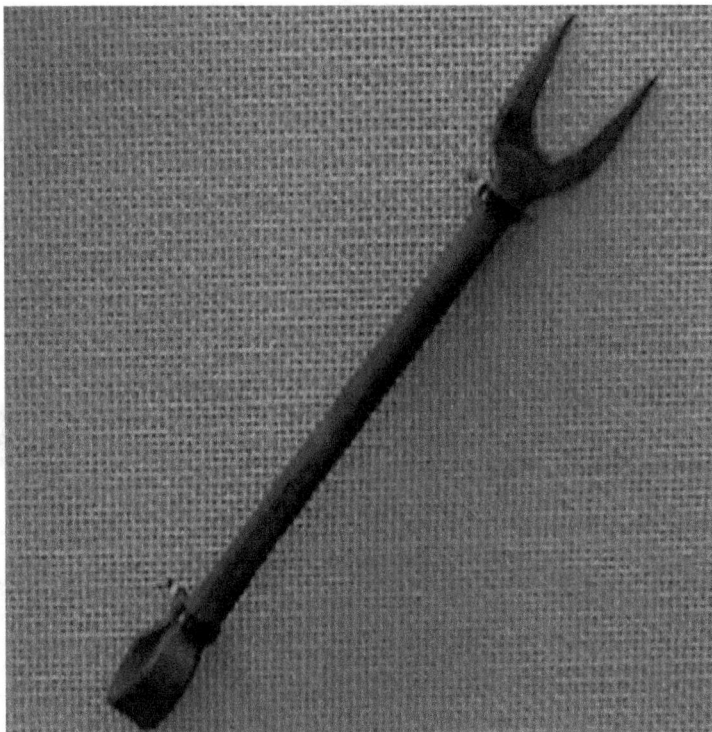

Tsubogiri model

Gantô

Gantô (龕燈) was a special lantern that different form the usual paper lanterns in Japan. They were made from hard material of wood or metal and with a device that kept the candle in a vertical position.

By using this type of lantern he could direct a beam of light and there was no need to extinguish the candle, just to turn the lantern towards the ground or a flat surface.

It is often associated with the *ninja* because it was such a great tool, so it was usually considered that a ganto was used for secret entry. In fact they probably did not use them so much, because of their sizes and clumsiness, the opposite to the *ninja* ideal.

Ninja preferred discrete and easy to carry tools. *Gantô* were used by government agents during the *Edo* Period.

Gantô model

Section of print

Kasugai and Tojimeki

These are tools used in construction work.

A *ninja* would use one to block a door; a necessary precaution if his presence wad discovered or to secure an area. In Japan doors are sliding doors, so ninja would use one to prevent an enemy entering.

The *kasugai* (鎹) had a horseshoe form and allowed them to block a door.

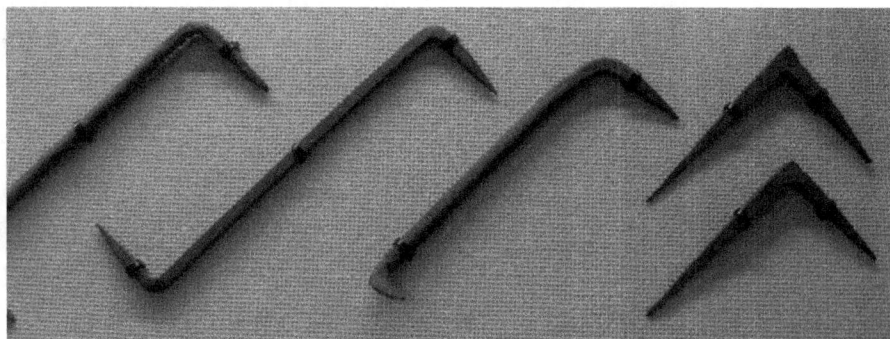

Kasugai models

Tojimeki (戸閉器) are used by putting it between sliding doors to seal them. Even doors made from rice paper and light wood were easy to break through, but the time it took to overcome the door lock and the need to break in gave a ninja the time to escape.

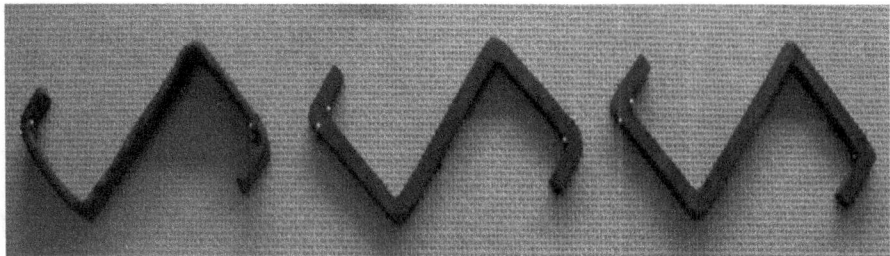

Tojimeki models

Lock picking tools

In japan sliding doors were clocked by latch, beams or blocks for which a saw would suffice, but when locks arrived from China and the West they placed an obstacle to ninja infiltration. So the *ninja* developed lock picking skills and the tools for it. Lock picking tools and master keys were used.

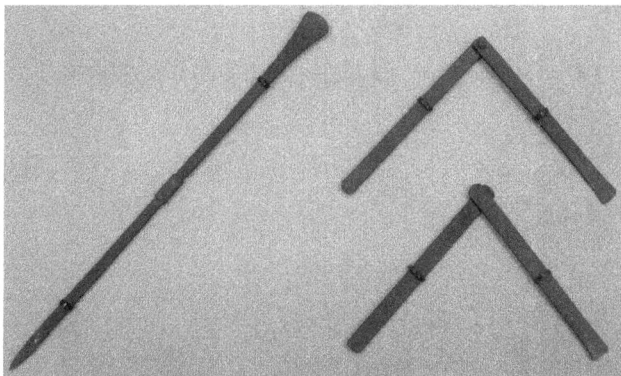

Tataminomi models

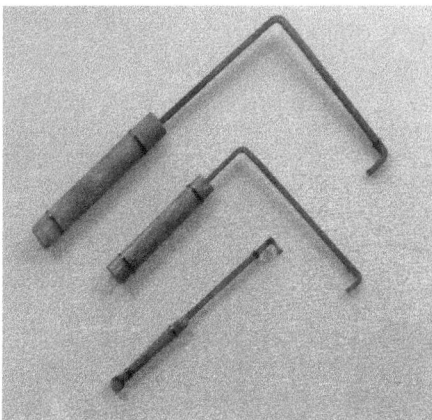

Kuroro kagi models

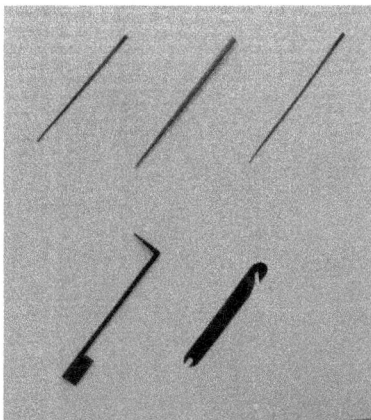

Saku models

Ladder and grapnel

If there was an obstacle is was often better to avoid it or climb over it.

Ninja used ladders of course but they were large and solid. So *ninja* developed their own type of ladder; flexible and light and easy to carry. Made from naturally light materials such as bamboo, light wood and rope it was easy to set up and conceal. A *ninja* had his own climbing skills to speed up the climb.

But some models of ladders are exaggerated in an attempt to impress the reader.

Grapnels were also used to surmount obstacles. A *ninja* could make one from a rope and sickle.

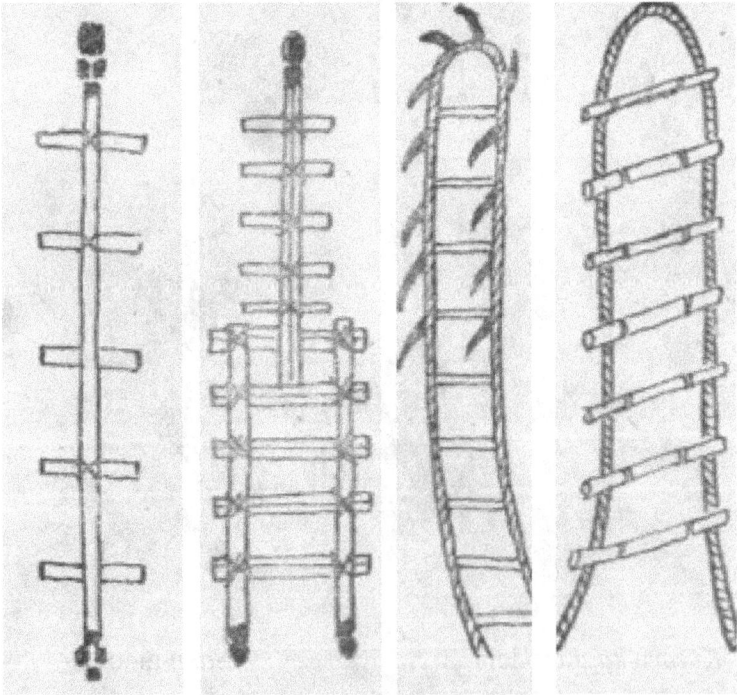

Ladders models

River crossing equipment

A river allowed a ninja to escape without trace and also cover long distances and as moats were constraints to infiltration the shinobi developed equipment for crossing water.

Mizugumo

Mizugumo (水蜘蛛), these 'water spiders' are the most famous *ninjutsu* equipment because they were described in *Mansenshukai*.

Yet the reality is the exact opposite because a *mizugumo* was absolutely not intended for crossing water, only on muddy ground or a swamp.

If he had to cross water it would be easier and quicker to swim because a *ninja* was an excellent swimmer.

In fact the mention of *mizugumo* in *Mansenshukai* is a typical deception by *ninjutsu* that required a *kuden* (secret oral communication) to be understood. The *mizugumo* was in reality a «*numa uki gutsu*» (沼浮沓), a set of wooden boards. Like a sandal a hole was put in for a lace, simpler to use.

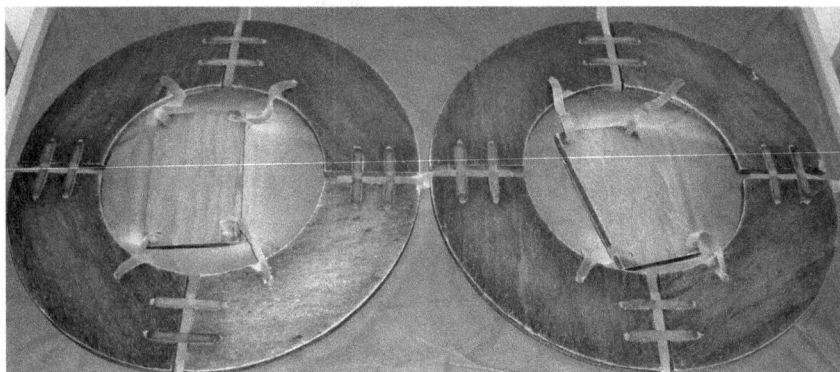

Reconstitution of mizugumo by mansenshûkai

The supposed way of utilising *Mizugumo*. But it's just imagination, in truth, *mizugumo* as described in *Mansenshukai*, was not used.

Rafts

The following illustrations show *ninja* ingenuity who made his own equipment from few items. We can see their cunning and improvisation similar to that for making ladders. Some ordinary rope, wooden board and materials are enough to make a useful raft.

Again we can see *ninja* creating their own equipment with the items they had to hand. As for ladders, it's probably again an attempt to impress like the usual rafts.

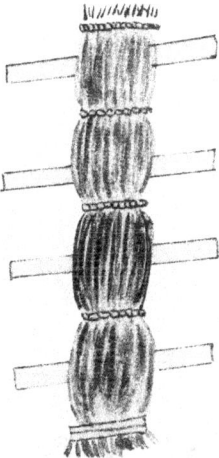

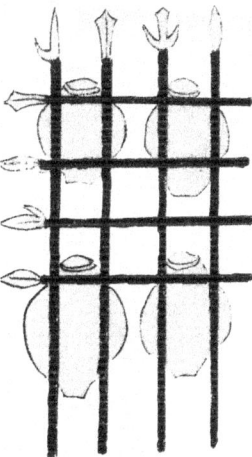

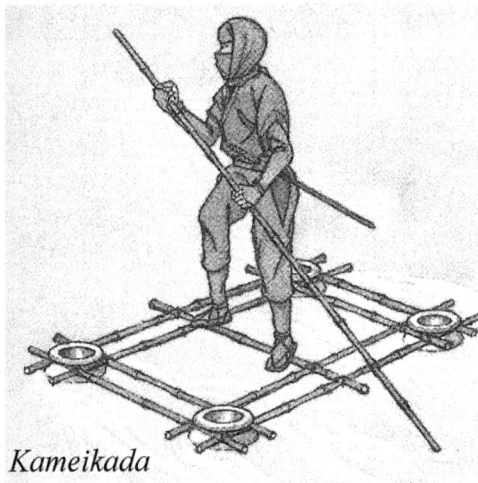

Gamaikada

Kameikada

Shinobibune

This is a boat, but the problem was its size, which the ninja solved. He made a collapsible folding boat.

The components were encased and waterproofed before use.

However the *Mansenshukai* description provokes doubt over how this boat could actually be used.

Reproduction of *shinobibune*

Associated *ninja* weapons

Ninjutsu was not a fighting discipline and supposed not to involve weapons, but some are inseparable from the ninja image. They following weapons are described to show their relationship to ninjutsu.

Shinobigatana

Shinobigatana, (忍び刀) : The term used for a *ninja* sword.

It is often said to have a short and straight blade but there is no way of conforming this and it is in fact a modern interpretation. In fact *ninja* preferred small compact items of equipment, so if he had to carry a weapon he would use a short and light one which gave him the advantage in a confined space. The *ninja* respected the use of a sword but it was identified with *samurai* and was thus of a different social status,

Utilisation of sword as footboard or detection tool

Bô

Bô, (棒) : Stick.

Sticks with hidden weapons eye points, blade or chains existed and are regarded incorrectly as exclusively *ninja* weapons.

There is the name «*shikomi tzue*» (仕込み杖), but it was not a *ninja* weapon, it appeared only at the and of the *Edo* period and the beginning of *Meiji* by which time *ninja* had ceased to exist.

Models of *Shikomi tzue*

Shuriken

Shuriken, (手裏剣) : Hand weapons for throwing.

These are the multi-pointed star and short nails or knives, the forms change with the schools and regions where they are employed. *Shuriken* are the weapons most closely associated with *ninja*, but there is no proof, and if a *ninja* had *shuriken* he would only have one or two.

The association of *ninja* with *shuriken* came from an old Japanese TV programme called *Onmitsu Kenshi*

Contrary to the usual idea of a *ninja shuriken*, they were not designed to kill or injure but to surprise an enemy and cause a diversion for his escape, a domain where the *ninja* excelled.

Historically *shuriken* were used by samurai and some martial art schools included *shuriken*, but now we see a strange situation ; Some bu-jutsu schools claiming they have links to ninjutsu because the curriculum of the school contain some shuriken-jutsu. It is a strange reverse of the historical situation!

Different models of *shuriken*

Kama and kusarigama

Kama (鎌), sickle a common farming implement used by the agricultural classes.

It is of course not a weapon, but when in the disguise of a farmer and coming under attack a *ninja* had only this tool to defend himself by.

The combination of sickle, chain and weight the kusarigama (鎖鎌) was frequently linked to the image of a *ninja*. But it was not a *ninja* weapon but a samurai weapon.

Kusiarigama had many sizes and variations, some models were quite small to benefit the use of the chain.

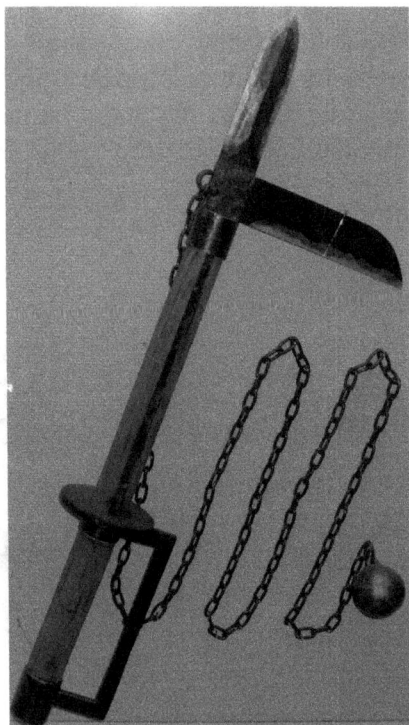

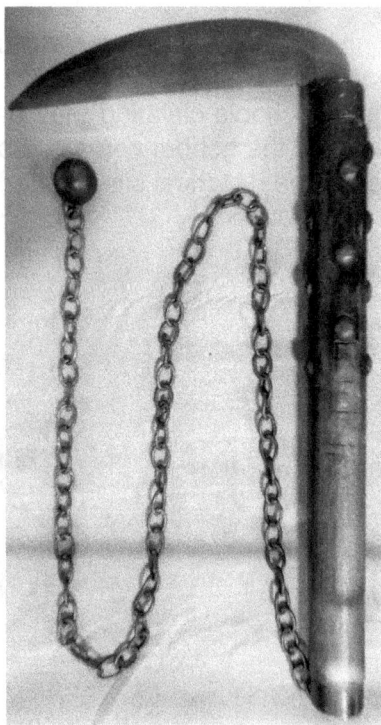

Reconstitution of models of *kusarigama*.
Notice the different position of chain

Tekken, tekkôkagi and kakute

Tekken

Tekken (鉄拳), iron fist. This was an iron device used to hit or to block an enemy blade, It was an ancestor of the American knuckleduster. It existed in many forms, some were sharp and others had spikes.

Tekkôkagi

Tekkôkagi (手甲鉤), claw. This instrument, often regarded as weapon, was in fact a climbing device.

Kakute

Kakute (角手) antler hand.

A ring with one or spikes, turned outside so it increased the injury when one hit or grabbed someone.

Once again it is important to mention that these objects could be found when the man was searched and reveal his mission so were not often used.

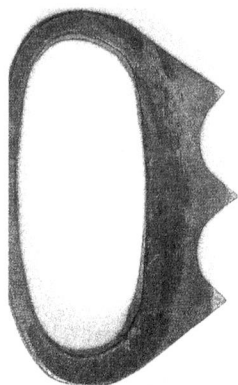

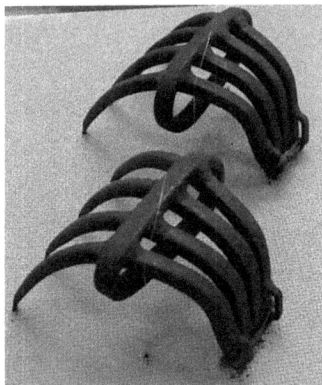

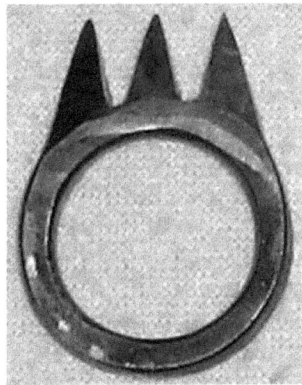

Tekken   *Tekkôkagi*   *Kakute*

Teppô

Teppô (鉄砲), musket.

Imported to Japan in 1543 by the Portuguese, this kind of weapon was despised by the samurai because it negated their warrior skills.

By contrast a gun could be used by *ninja* without hindrance, they had no objections to their use.

Ninja probably used *kaihô* (芥砲) too, a light and portable version.

Although easy to conceal and use a gun was very noisy and compromising when a ninja was searched. To use a *kaihô* was equivalent to raising the alarm so it was used sparingly.

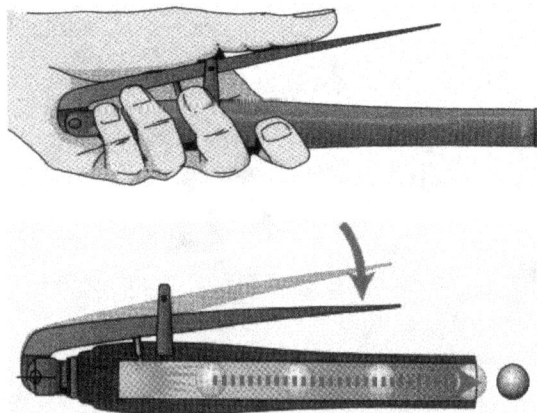

*Kaihô, lever is
a trigger to
provoke fire*

Ninjutsu and its relation to the natural world

Ninjutsu was not born in a dôjô or in a school but developed in and was closely connected to the natural environment. The observation of nature was the basis of many techniques.

Learning from nature

In general, the basis of *ninja* wisdom was the observation of nature. The spirit of *ninjutsu* came from this link with nature and had an influence on the direction it took.

The observation of nature and natural phenomena gave birth to certain disciplines such as knowledge of plants, weather forecasting and topography.

Ninjutsu is an art of survival and in particular surviving alone in the natural world. So a *ninja* had a deep understanding of the laws of nature and would not fight against them.

Sharp senses, developed intuition and relation to the divine were important parts of *ninjutsu*.

The *ninja* would practise retreating into nature looking for wild and quiet places in order to perfect his skills and develop his spirituality.

Some tourist places in Japan today are known to have been important for *ninja* training in the past.

Learning from animals

Many animal species have a natural aptitude to delude and escape from predators. They inspired *ninjutsu* techniques.

The following strategies were used by *ninja*, probably after the observation and imitation of forest dwellers, so the names of the techniques came directly from the animals that inspired them, although it is possible that some are a modern attribution.

- *Uzura gakure* (ウズラ隠れ) ; hiding like a quail

Just as a quail hides behind a stone or obstacle, shrinking into itself.

- *Tanuki gakure* (タヌキ隠れ) ; hiding like a badger

A Japanese badger climbs a tree to hide and escape

- *Kitsune gakure* (キツネ隠れ) ; hiding like a fox

Like a fox crossing water to erase it odour.

Many other animals use other kinds of strategies, covering themselves with leaves, soil etc.

A *ninja* never forgot what animals taught him.

View of *Handôzan*, a training place for *ninja*

The scientific spirit of ninjutsu

Although it is an unknown or forgotten part of ninjutsu, it is important to recall that ninjutsu contributed to scientific research. A practical mind and sense of inspiration were advantageous on a mission. The following examples illustrate this unknown aspect of ninjutsu.

The technological arsenal

Gunpowder

Ninja didn't wait for the importation of fire weapons for the mastery of gunpowder, *kayaku* (火薬) and its different applications.

It had a relation with Japan because gunpowder was invented in China which had relations with Japan from time immemorial.

So *ninja* always had experiments and developed various techniques using gunpowder to prepare an arsenal that was ahead of its time :

Torinoko (鳥の子) : A smoke bomb to aid disappearance.

Noroshi (烽火) : Includes gunpowder for sending messages.

Hyakurai jû (百雷銃) : Successive exploding sets.

Umebi (埋め火) : Explosive mine.

Hôrokyuha (焙烙火矢) : Explosives.

Hiya (火矢) : Rocket arrow

 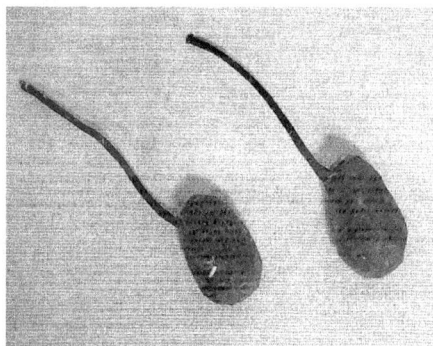

Torinoko

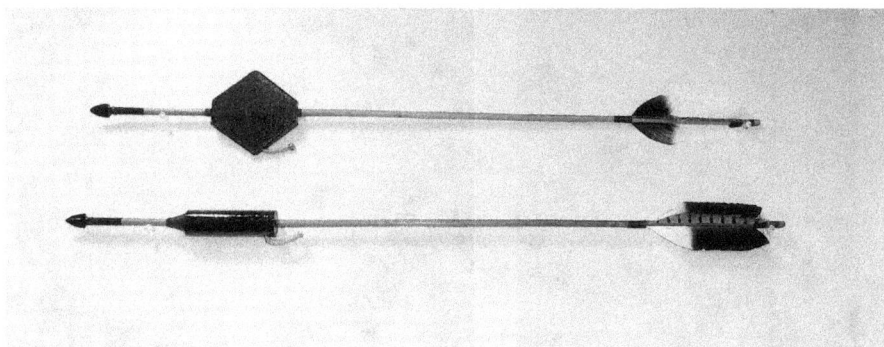

Hiya

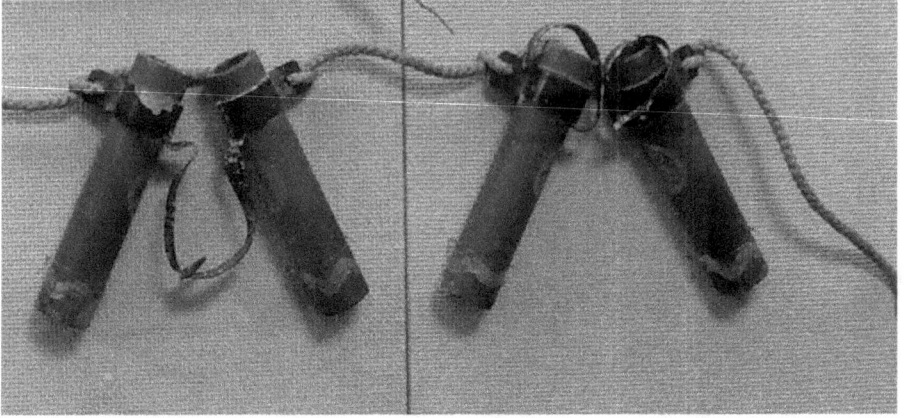

Hyakurai jû

Noroshidsutsu, receiving
noroshi preparation

Reconstitution of *horoku-hya*, explosive

Lighting

The ingenuity of *ninja* led to lighting systems and specific torches for missions

Tanagokoro taimatsu
Tanagokoro taimatsu (掌松明). This was easy to carry and conceal because it was smaller than the palm of one's hand. It was used to search in the darkest places

Suichû taimatsu
Suichû taimatsu (水中松明), a secret compound based on gunpowder that was a water resistant torch.

Yoshitsune taimatsu
Yoshitsune Taimatsu (義 経 松明) is a lantern made from a hollowed bovine horn, which is soaked in a preparation which, interacting with the horn emits a glow. This type of torch is supposed to be waterproof too.

Tanagokoro taimatsu

Suichû taimatsu

The chemical arsenal

The *ninja* pharmacopeia

Through his contact with nature the *ninja* developed a deep knowledge of pharmacopeia. This allowed him to prepare a wide range of substances, there was influence from China too with its own tradition of pharmacopeia.

His mastery of pharmacopeia and ability to crate medicines allowed him to keep in excellent health, a permanent concern for the *ninja*. Also a *ninja* could double as a medicine seller.

The making of poisons was a key skill in *ninjutsu*. Many applications were possible, to kill, to make ill, to simulate illness.

If the *Iga* region was known to be associated with black powder, the region of *Kôka* was equally famous for his mastery of the pharmacopoeia. The art of poison (*dokukai*) was there too and as, well developed.

Today, moreover, many pharmaceutical enterprises are located in *Kôka*.

The knowledge of edible plants allow shinobi to survive alone when he had to escape and withdraw into nature.

Some types of *ninja* preparations :

Torikabuto (鳥兜), flower for poisons

Dokudami (蕺草), a plant that is an antidote to poison

Ichô (銀杏), the leaf as used for a tonic, the seed of relaxation.

Senburi (千振), a plant to aid digestion and also as a filterer for eater.

Ikarisô (虎杖), for vitality.

I*tadori* (虎杖), used for pain relief.

Torikabuto

Ikariso

Ichô (Ginkgo)

Senburi

Itadori

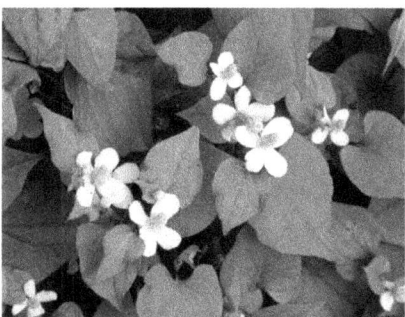

Dokudami

The pharmacopeia was not limited to plants but involved animals too.

For example, *ninja* collected worms commonly found in latrines. They were dried and grilled and turned into powder.
The powder had an effect on sleep.

Wolf dung was used in *noroshi* because of it smoke-inducing properties.

Snake venom was of course important for poison.

Preparations and chemical reactions

In addition to medicines and poisons the *ninja* used specific preparations with different applications to help him in his missions.

Ninja used some substances to limit the effect of alcohol on an individual when he had to drink it.
He used another product to accelerate the effects of alcohol. It was put secretly into someone's cup.

To saw through something silently the *ninja* would put a sticky substance on to the saw.

The *ninja* had knowledge of the exothermic reaction produced by mixing different elements. The mixture was put into a sealed box and used as a body warmer and to preserve the fingers's abilities.

Another kind of mixture could creature a diversion by producing smoke when thrown into water.

Common Ninja Techniques

During the course of their information gathering and spying missions the ninja used a wide range of skills and techniques. The following are some of particular use.

Tenmon and *chiri* environmental strategies

These two disciplines are an integral part of ninja formation, they were about using and surviving in the natural world, one foundation of ninjutsu

Tenmon

Tenmon (天文), is a discipline involving the determination of the weather by the observation of the sky, the moon, stars etc, …

The weather had a direct effect on missions out of doors and it was essential to predict it. For example, it was useless to take along a fire weapon if it was going to rain. At the same time rain could aid infiltration.

That is why a ninja was familiar with the signs of meteorology. Cloud formations or animal reactions were among the things the ninja studied.

Chiri

Chiri (地理), this is concerned with topography.

In spying and information gathering map recognition and ground observation were essential elements.

A *ninja*, by the nature of his craft, tried to create advantages and disadvantages of the ground to prepare a journey, make an ambush, set up fortifications etc. At a personal level he needed to know the location of springs and plants to survive himself.

Tonhô survival strategy

Ninjutsu was above all the art of survival. Accordingly an important part was hiding and escaping. These strategies called tondo permitted him to cover his flight and avoid capture by all means at his disposal. It was imperative for a ninja to report back on mission. The diversity and importance of escape techniques prove that the arts of combat were far from the spirit of ninjutsu. For a ninja flight was the key to victory. These nomenclatures for classifying techniques are probably modern, which does not however rule out the ninja have used all these elements.

Using the five elements
The *gotonhô* (五遁法) technique involved the five elements of Chinese tradition ; wood, fire, earth, water, iron.

Each could be used to aid escape, for example :

- Wood (木) ; hide behind a tree
- Fire (火) ; use fire as a diversion
- Earth (土) ; hide in a hole in the ground or cover yourself with earth.
- Water (水) ; hide in a lake or throw water in the faces of pursuers.
- Iron or gold : from the Idea of (gold) dazzling by sun's reflection on a polished surface.

The following three techniques were grouped as *ten chi jin* (天地人) : *Ten* (天) use the weather, *Chi* (地) use the environment, *Jin* (人) use people. *Ten chi jin* is a common classification system in Japan.

Using meteorology

With his skills in meteorology the *ninja* used different manifestations of the weather to his own advantage.

Tentonjuhô (天遁十法), the ten meteorological factors covered escape : Sun (*nitton* 日遁), moon (*getton* 月遁), stars (*seiton* 星遁), clouds (*unton* 雲遁), fog (*muton* 霧遁), thunder (*raiton* 雷遁), lightning (*denton* 電遁), wind (*fûton* 風遁), rain (*uton* 雨遁), snow (*setton* 雪遁).

Using the environment

Chitonjuhô (地遁十法), the ten factors in the environment to aid flight. They are : Trees (*mokuton* 木遁), grass (*sôton* 草遁), fire (*katon* 火遁), smoke (*enton* 煙遁), earth (*doton* 土遁), buildings (*okuton* 屋遁), iron or gold (*kinton* 金遁), stone (*sekiton* 石遁), water (*suiton* 水遁), hot water(*tôton* 湯遁).

Using people and animals

With his skills at mind control the *ninja* could use people to hide him or to flee. These strategies are *jintonjûhô* (人遁十法), ten ways of using people to cover flight : Man (*danton* 男遁), woman (*jôton* 女遁), old people (*rôton* 老遁), young people (*yôton* 幼遁), aristocrats (*kiton* 貴遁), outcasts (*senton* 賤遁).

Animals were used for diversion or their effect of on people such as : Birds (*kinton* 禽遁), animal (*jûton* 獣遁), insects (*chûton* 虫遁), fish (*gyoton* 魚遁).

Fumigation

Enton (煙遁), involving escape under cover of smoke and also to give a supernatural impression.

Disguise

Hensôjutsu (変装術). Using disguise to escape or infiltrate (see next chapter.)

Hensôjutsu disguise techniques

As part of his mission a *ninja* could adopt another identity, even to develop comic capabilities to avoid arousing suspicion.

Of course the nature of the mission determined the disguise but seven types, *shichi hôde* (七方出) were frequently used :

- *Shukke* (出家) ; monk.

    Involved knowing the Buddhist doctrines and sutra.

- Yamabushi (山伏) ; monk

    A monk who practised *shugendô* (asceticism discipline).

- *Sarugakushi* (猿楽師) : Actor

    Comic or artistic acting.

- *Hôkashi* (放下師) : Entertainer

    In street performance such as acrobatics.

- *Shônin* (商人) : Peddlar

    An itinerant merchant with his stall.

- *Tsune no katachi* (常の形) : Ordinary person.

    A farmer or samurai

Shukke   *Yamabushi*   *Komusô*

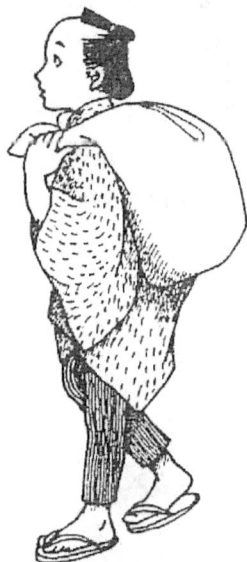

Sarugakushi   *Shônin*   *hôkashi*   *Tsune no kata*

The seven disguises presented certain advantages in different situations :

As a pedlar, artist or entertainer the *ninja* was directly in contact with the population so he could collect or spread news and information.

More specifically as an artist or entertainer he had to deliver an authentic professional performance.

During the *Sengoku* Period for example, the *Nô* theatre was very popular with daimyo so it was a very good opportunity to approach them under the guise of a *sarugakushi.*

Itinerant persons justified their presence in village without any suspicion. A *ninja* who assumed these disguises over an unbroken period of many years attained a masterly level in them.

During the time of civil wars passes are needed to cross the borders because frontiers were always closed.

Priest and monks could usually pass without difficulties and some of them were itinerant, conveying correspondence between temples etc.,

The *yamabushi* and *komusô*, carried swords to protect themselves against bandits on the road, although this was an exceptional case because monks were not warriors.

To assume that disguise a *ninja* needed a perfect knowledge of rituals, divination and the sutras. Under disguise as a *komusô* he would play the *shakuhachi* (flute).

The final identity was that of an ordinary person, but whatever identity he adopted the *ninja* had to have a deep understanding of the region he claimed to come from, its fashion, dialect and local history to be believed. Because borders are closed in feudal Japan a strong regional identity developed.

It is important to understand that disguise was but one small part of *hensôjutsu.*

If he had to take on a role his behavior had to change completely depending upon the social class : A *ninja* disguised as a farmer would speak on equal terms with another farmer but deferred before a *samurai* or noble from a superior class. There was no place for a quick reaction that would arouse suspicion.

To illustrate this we may consider the anecdote which may be true or not of Minamoto Yoshitsune, a historical person often regarded as a *ninja* and his servant and bodyguard Benkei, During their flight Yoshitsune was disguised as a servant in the party in which he travelled. While waiting to cross a border they are challenged by a guard, whereby Benkei quickly reacted by hitting his master and insulting him. The guard was convinced and let them pass. After passing the guard post Benkei is said to have been wiling to die, but Yoshitsune only laughed. He had been surprised by his bodyguard's reaction but considered that the trick was an excellent one.

In addition to being disguised a *ninja* could imitate a mendicant or a physically disabled person. It is not surprising to learn that a *ninja* could simulate physical disability such as a limp, a loose limb or by using fish scales even blindness.

Similarly a *ninja* could change his appearance. Change hair style, growing a beard, changing his facial and bodily appearance. Other details could be used to avoid recognition.

Bôjutsu, mind manipulation

As a spy information collection was a *ninja*'s duty and the reason for the existence of *ninjutsu*.

The popular impression is of someone moving in the shadows of the night, seen by nobody, acting without being noticed.
This is *Innin* (陰忍) part of ninja's activity.

In fact a *ninja* operated mainly during the day with direct contact to the people he needed to approach for receiving information about his mission.
This is the y*ônin* (陽忍) part of ninja's activity.

For this the most useful component of ninjutsu was the mastery of the art of mind manipulation ; *bôjutsu* (謀術).

This included sowing discord within a group, affecting everyone's mind and actions while collecting information while being completely unnoticed.

Knowing psychology a *ninja* could immediately decipher the character of people and take advantage of it, corrupting or taking advantage of important people.

Gosha no jutsu (五車の術) is a technique of mind control using five psychological levers :

1- *Kissha* (喜車), happiness
Make friends with the person, flatter him and give him presents.

2- *Dosha* (怒車), anger

Make him angry by provoking decisions and acting inconsiderately.

3 - *Aisha* (哀車), sadness

Using the sadness of other people to comfort him in sorrow and giving him unearned consideration.

4 - *Rakusha* (楽車), by conviction

Convince a person, change his convictions and join his cause.

5 - *Kyousha* (恐車), scaring

Frighten the person and alter his mind state.

Kunoichi no jutsu are of course the mind control techniques of ninja.

One can see the true capability of nine through his intelligence, cunning and ingenuity. It was the most frightening of all ninja techniques ; manipulation.

By manipulation the ninja could win without a fight.

Kunoichi no jutsu the manipulation of desire

It is often said that the expression «*kunoichi*» refers to female *ninja*, but it has a specific meaning in Japanese.

The three constituent syllable using the three different syllabaries write kunoichi as くノー.

When put together make the kanji ; 女 for woman.

In reality *kunoichi* does not indicate a female *ninja*; *ninjutsu* training was hard and women did not take part in it. It refers instead to a *ninja* using attraction for his own advantage.

Consequently, the term *kunoichi* can be applied equally to man or woman whose charms are used, even if these people are not aware of being manipulated by a *ninja*.

Kunoichi no jutsu (くノーの術) therefore has to be understood as the manipulation of someone's sensual desires to achieve a mission.

Putting someone in this position allows easier infiltration, even if the person is unaware of the role they are employing.

Dentatsu jutsu, communication strategy

It is equally important when spying to collect information and to protect it in the case of interception. The protection of his secrets was a constant worry for a ninja so he developed secure means of communication.

Slang
Slang, *ingo* (隠語), into was practised by people within the same group to secure a conversation and prevent others from understanding what was said if they eavesdropped.

Slang constantly changed so as not to allow the slightest chance for an outsider to become familiar with it.

Hidden messages
Ninja used hidden message that only people who were used to the practice could find and interpret.

A rope or thin cord *yuinawa* (結縄) placed in a specific position made a specific signal.

Otherwise plant seeds or rice grains of different colours or arrangements sent messages.

Distant communication
Many methods were used to develop and perfect long distance communications. *Ninja* principally used a code based on flags and smoke signals (*noroshi*) for transmitting messages over a distance. During the night he would use a torches or lanterns (*gantô,* ...).

Passwords
To formally authenticate a contact passwords and pre-agreed recognition sigs *aikotoba* (合言葉) would be necessary. The *ninja* used many passwords, some based on association (sea/mountain, moon/sun etc).

Warifu (割符), a decorated piece of wood was used. It was cut into two halves ; two people meeting can assemble and authenticate the other when they met.

The spirituality of *ninjutsu*

A deep spirituality is present within ninjutsu that is clearly distinguishable from professional activity and may be understood in its own right.

Spirituality, as a component of ninjutsu, derives from two important factors : history and necessity.

In historical terms ninjutsu of course reflects its time and mentality. Even though it would be difficult to prove nowadays, to experts ninjutsu was closely tied to Shinto.
This is not surprising when we consider that Shinto is the indigenous religion of Japan and that ninjutsu took shape at a time when important meetings, decisions and actions were decided in temples or after rituals to gain benefits and blessings from the gods.

In this regard ninjutsu is not exceptional in Japan. The origins and development of the tradition were certainly decided after being submitted for the approval of the gods in their shrines. Some of this is explicitly mentioned in ninjutsu denshô.

Secondly, necessity played an important role in the spirituality of the ninja. It is well-known that when times are hard religion and spirituality act in parallel to help each other.

It was the same in Japan in the course of long and bloody times of war lasting many centuries. In times of violence the law of the strong is dominant and everything is grasped in order to survive, even recourse to the gods to beg their special protection, advice or strengths.

In this context spiritual or esoteric practices (as kujigoshinhô) have a logical place, not only through their use by ninja but spread throughout Japanese society : Samurai, daimyo, monks ascetic practitioners etc to lead military and religious activities.

So the ninja, who constantly lived with a 'Sword of Damocles' hanging over his head (one of the meanings of the kanji non) integrated the many spiritual practices in his training with his conept of the universe.

Thus spiritual practice was of great importance in ninjutsu practice and the intense way the ninja practised it because it was a matter of life or death, it assured him that he would surpass his mental and physical limitations. He would endure the hard ninjutsu training and have success on his missions.

These intensely practised rituals played a significant role on the acquisition of a strong mental state among ninja who developed these capacities to last till the end of his missions, It is important to not that esoteric practices were abandoned (other than in some religious establishments) during the Edo Period, a time of peace.

Views of *Aekuni* sanctuary, present in *ninjutsu* tradition

Views of *Akame*, high place of *ninjutsu* training in old times. A place that is wild and difficult of access, also a perfect isolated place, for retirement. Reaching this place was a part of training, so hard and difficult were the roads.

Fudôshin

This notion is inextricably linked to the *ninja*. He had to reach through his training *fudôshin* (不動心), meaning ; «an immovable heart».

This principle, one of the most important in *ninjutsu*, implies a mental state where the heart and its emotions were fully controlled and would not be troubled by events, or even immediate danger.

It allowed him for example to not let through any emotion in case of suspicion, not to flinch even when threatened by a sword blade, mastering his emotions and keeping his self control in check.

Not letting his judgements and actions be controlled by emotions and not acting without consideration.

The notion of *fudôshin* can be understood using the kanji «*shinobi*» where the heart and emotions are under the control of a sword (a vigilant spirit).

The existence of this concept in *ninjutsu* is proof of the importance of mental training for a *ninja*.

Ninja no sanbyô

Using all his resources for a missions, a *ninja* cannot allow a weakening physical or mental condition to obstruct it.

So *ninja* mastered the preparation of medicines. But also the ninja followed strict mental training to keep his emotions under control, to be credible when adopting another identity, and not to let distracting thoughts - fatal in decision making - affect the situation in an emergency.

By tradition three "diseases" were the worst enemies of ninja

- *Osore* (恐れ) ; fear, paralysed the body and spirit
- *Anadori* (侮り) ; arrogance, blocked the spirit
- *Kangaesugi* (考え過ぎ) ; too much thought, blocked intuition.

Ninja had to stay constantly vigilant not to allow these negative emotions enter his mind and influence him.

These three diseases were really harmful to a *ninja* because they interfered with his spirituality, broke his link with the divine, an essential part of *ninjutsu*. And then, these diseases lead him to fail a mission.

Fear, arrogance and over-thinking represented a dark side, a blocking of the calm spirit that should be untroubled.

Because his rigorous training set him above the common people it is clear that a *ninja*'s greatest enemy could be himself without being aware of it.

Here again we see the meaning of the kanji *shinobi*.

Kuji goshinhô

Kuji goshinhô (九字護身法), literally «the nine seals for protection» is a famous practice associated with the *ninja* image, again from its representation in *kabuki*.

Kuji goshinho, represents only a small part of the disciple of invocation, protection and surpassing one's limits. As noted in the introduction to the chapter, those practices were not exclusive to the *ninja*.

The practice of *kuji goshinho* consisted of creating special forms in a specific order using the position of one's hands.

The roots if the practice probably came from India via China become settling and spreading in Japan. The origins of the signs came in great part from sanskrit, the sacred language of India. The position of the hands as a sign would represent in a graphical form the signs of the sanskrit alphabet.

The nine seals as pronounced and performed are as follows:

臨 - *rin*   兵 - *hyô*   闘 - *tô*

者 - *sha*   皆 - *kai*   陣 - *jin*

列 - *retsu*   在 - *zai*   前 - *zen*

The seals of *kuji goshinhô* are done in this order (Note that the following is with the style of reading Japanese ; from right to left).

Sha   Tô   Pyô   Rin

Zen   Zai   Retsu   Jin   Kai

A simpler and faster version of *kuji goshinhô* was called *kuji kiri* (九字きり) ; the cut of nine seals.

This method consisted of drawing with ones fingers the top horizontal and vertical lines 5 by 4.

Every line represented a seal and is symbolically written using the cutting motion of the finger.

This is a representation of the realisation of *kuji kiri*, starting form the upper left side, drawing a successively a horizontal and a vertical line.

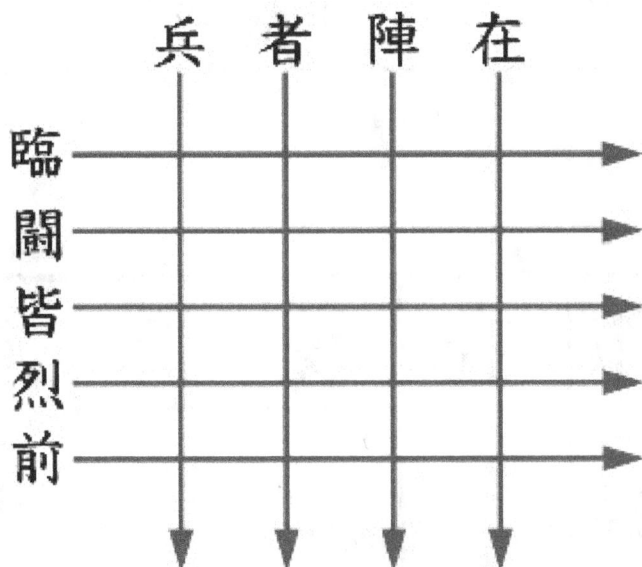

兵　者　陣　在

臨　闘　皆　烈　前

Jujigoshinhô

Words have meaning and every meaning carries a specific energy (*ki*). That is why a ninja facing certain situations would write a kanji with the desired meaning to achieve his goals.

He would write the kanji on his hand and bring it to his mouth to absorb the effect.

This practice was *jûjigoshinhô* (十字後辛護身法), the ten signs for proaction, but variations exist.

天 (Sky)

To give self assurance.
The sky is above everything from the sky everything is of equal size

龍 (Dragon)

To cross water safely.
The dragon is associated with water in Asia

虎 (Tiger)

To cross wild plains safely.
The tiger is an animal associated with wild nature there are no tigers in Japan, hence the foreign origins.

王 (King)

Having the power to accomplish a goal.
The king unifies heaven and earth he is favoured by the heavens and can accomplish great things.

命 (Life)

Avoid poison.
To have the life power to resist poison.

勝 (Victory)

To cross over obstacles and succeed.
Success os the only object in a ninja mission, so it is a most appropriate kanji.

是 (Justice)

To cure and restore health.
In Japan disease is seen as a violation of the natural order because health is the natural state. It is just to be in good condition.

鬼 (Demon)

Affirm ones life spirit.
Don't be affected by fear, have the strength of a demon

水 (Water)

The purifying spirit.
Universally water has the power to purify someone who bathes in it in body and spirit.

大 (Great)

Intensify emotions and energies.
Develop positive feelings and energy.

Books about Ninjutsu

(NB ; the following books are known by the titles Bansenshukai, Shô-ninki and Ninpiden, but these are modern readings of the kanji and they are written here using the original readings. These documents famous for their treatment of ninjutsu are famous in the West so it is necessary to establish their true nature.

Ninjutsu was an exclusively oral tradition including secret transmission within ninja families. That is why it appears so strange and leads to speculation as to why some ninja would write complete books about it.

To set it in context, it is important to appreciate that the following texts were written during the Edo Period when ninjutsu was experiencing a rapid decline after its peak during the preceding Sengoku era. In this exceptional era an exceptional decision was made to write texts and books to praise the ninja's capacity and to influence potential employees. These documents exaggerated things to evoke admiration and respect.

So these documents, regarded as long lasting ninjutsu tradition and preserving it were not written for that at all.

In reality it is more a question of finding anything authenti. Planned to be shown to future employers the texts were hidden in code so that no one except a ninja who received the kuden (oral transmission) could understand the real meaning.

No written transmission was added by anyone who has received the kuden. So even today the true meaning of the texts is still unknown. This applies to every text concerning ninja and ninjutsu.

Moreover it is important to understand the mentality of the Edo Period. It was deeply influenced by the classical culture and values of China and was radically different from other periods in this respect.

There was a large discrepancy between what ninjutsu and ninja really were and reports about them made in the Edo Period, the time of their dispersion and the time when the texts were marked by new ideas and values.

In edition, spying was delegated to samurai who had no interest in it up to that point and tried to see it as a noble activity that fitted in with their core values.

Because of this we can appreciate that the authors of the Edo period ninjutsu documents were not ninja nor did they come from ninja families. Because it was a secret tradition ninjutsu was equivalent to the family silver, passed on from generation to generation, never revealed and preferably lost rather than preserved.

To reiterate, even when they were in charge of spying missions samurai were not ninja nor were they trained in ninjutsu. It was an oral tradition so it was totally absurd to think that ninjutsu can be learned from books, even in its incorrect form.

Mansenshûkai (萬川集海)

The title can be translated as " The ocean formed by ten thousand rivers". It is a text written under the name Fujibayashi Yasutake of 1676, officially to preserve the *ninja* tradition.

Mansenshûkai is presented in an encyclopedic form about *ninjutsu*. The title makes a reference to *ninja* lineages and *ninja* schools.

Mansenshûkai is often called the «bible of *ninjutsu*». It was used by the Intelligence Services during World War II.

However, contrary to appearances, this document would not have been written by *ninja* but by a *heigakusha* (practical military strategist) who took the initiative to produce the compilation with the agreement and perhaps the help of *ninja* families to help them canvas potential employers.

Mansenshûkai is the most eloquent testimony of the rapid and certain decline of *ninja* activities during the *Edo* Period, rather than being an exhaustive book about *ninjutsu* as a secret tradition.

The author, of course, presents spying as a *ninja* activity but adds many subjects and topics beyond this simple activity such as strategy, moral attitude, rituals, astronomy, equipment etc, ... It shows that *ninjutsu* exists in a wide field of culture.

Obviously *Mansenshûkai* depends on *kuden* without which the descriptions of poisons and explosives would not work. This is intended to thwart the user who would try it without the secret knowledge.

Mizugumo is an excellent example : Authentic *ninja* equipment (*numa uki gutsu*) is evoked under a different form and name (*mizugumo*) to keep the secret. The whole of *Mansenshûkai* is written in this vein, although it is possible that the author did not know the *kuden* because he was not linked to the *ninja* tradition.

Seininki (正忍記)

This can be translated as «Authentic writings about *ninjutsu*». It was written by Masataka Natori (under the pseudonym of Fuji Issuishi) in 1681.

The work was promoted incorrectly during the *Showa* Period as a ninja writing.

In reality the author was a *samurai* and his school, the *Natori-ryû*, was a *samurai* school and not *ninjutsu*. Because of this we must be careful about using the terms *ninja* and *ninjutsu* in this context.

By asserting his skills at *ninjutsu* he was attempting to ennoble it. Here is a *samurai* trying to legitimise his new spying role, and trying to link it to a tradition that was not a *samurai* one until the *Edo* Period.

Following the fashion of the times, the author linked *ninjutsu* to the famous Chinese «Art of War» by Sun Tzu, which was very popular among the *samurai* class of the *Edo* era trying throughout to give a definition of *shinobi* that was consistent with the new moral values of Japanese society.

The book requires *kuden* too, for a true understanding.

Shinobihiden (忍秘伝)

This can be translated «Secret writings about *ninjutsu*».

It is said that it was begun in 1560, but its attribution to Hattori Hanzo immediately poses questions about the date. In fact, probably, many people collaborated in writing it.

So the supposed ancient date is probably no more than an attempt to pretend that something is older than it really is.

In addition to advice about ninja missions, this writing exposes like the *Mansenshûkai*, some tools and equipment for missions : Saws, rafts, hooks, sickles are mentioned with ideas about their size and mode of use.

Of course, *kuden* are required too.

Conclusion

We are at the end of this book. I hope to have shed some light on *ninjutsu*, an overlooked tradition but one that has an incredible richness and scope. This recognition of *ninjutsu* was delayed because of its reputation in folklore and theatre, which was systematically linked to it and discredited it for serious research.

But now there is excellent news that things are changing. Mie University in Japan opened in 2012 a research section about the *ninjutsu* tradition. This department, unique in the world, is directed by Professor Yuji Yamada and assures the recognition and legitimacy of *ninjutsu* through a valid historical approach in Japanese culture.

Mie University has benefitted from Master Jinichi Kawakami's collaboration. As the last heir to the *ninjutsu* tradition, his knowledge is essential to strip the veil from the secrets of the *ninjutsu* tradition.

Mie university's research purpose is nothing less than to change our actual vision of *ninjutsu* for a real historical approach.

As for it being a Japanese tradition it is necessary to have a deep undemanding of Japanese culture before passing judgement on *ninjutsu*.

If this work helps in that I will consider that its objective has been achieved.

Guillaume Lemagnen.

Acknowledgements

I am indebted to everyone who brought their help directly and indirectly to the production of this book.

First, I want to thank mister Jinichi Kawakami, master in bujutsu and specialist in *ninjutsu* tradition, for his interest to my work. His corrections, advice and support were essential.

Professor Yuji Yamada, historian at Mie university. The research he supervises in partner with mister Kawakami will have a great repercussion on the future for the recognition of this tradition.

Mr Ikeda, authentic searcher and passionate of ninjutsu, for his pertinent advice and his tireless desire to share his passion.

Mr Yasushi Kiyomoto, a close disciple of master Kawakami, for his revealing explanations.

Mr Masaru Nakahira, for his encouragements and help.

Mr Yonezawa Norihiko enthusiastic researcher of ninjutsu, specialist of ancient history and environment.

Iga Ninja Museum, where some photos came from.

I cannot quote everyone here, but I want to thanks all people of Mie prefecture who brought me help.

And I want to thanks specially M. Bernard Bordas, French independent researcher, specialist of world martial tradition and Japan warrior tradition, funder of the ninjutsu museum in France. Without him nothing would be possible.